Tapfuma Gutsa
Melancholy Girl 1988

CONTEMPORARY STONE CARVING *from* ZIMBABWE

22 JULY - 25 NOVEMBER 1990

Exhibition supported by:

NATIONAL ARTS COUNCIL OF ZIMBABWE
VISITING ARTS OFFICE OF GREAT BRITAIN AND NORTHERN IRELAND
HENRY MOORE FOUNDATION

PATRONS: ANGLO AMERICAN CORPORATION, ERF LIMITED, PETER GABRIEL, STANDARD CHARTERED BANK, CLUFF RESOURCES plc, GENERAL ELECTRIC CO plc.

ISBN 1 871480 04 3

Designed by Ian Holmes
Photographs at the YSP by Jerry Hardman-Jones

Front cover:

Bernard Matemera
Great Spirit Woman 1982

Previous page:

Nicholas Mukomberanwa
The Corrupting Power of Money 1985

CONTENTS

Opposite:
Stone carving in the Vukutu landscape, Zimbabwe.
Photograph by Frank McEwen

A number of the artists also recognise the importance of the influential Joram Mariga, a sculptor who is reputed to be one of the first artists in Zimbabwe to carve soapstone; an inspiration and example to many he is often referred to as the Father of Shona Sculpture. Nor must we forget Tom Blomefield, the ex tobacco farmer, who founded the sculptors' community in Tengenenge. Now a place of pilgrimage, Tengenenge has been, and continues to be, the home of many of the important sculptors in Zimbabwe.

The exhibition is not intended as an historical survey and although fairly comprehensive, (thirty-six sculptors representing the more established early masters along with new vital and articulate younger sculptors), I am aware that there are gaps; so we must give due recognition to those talented and important artists who, for various reasons, could not be included in this exhibition. Nevertheless, it is the largest open air exhibition of stone carving from Zimbabwe ever to be assembled and without the hard work, determination, cooperation and enthusiasm of our friends in Zimbabwe it would never have happened. It is by any standards an event which exemplifies international cooperation and understanding.

From the outset the dynamic Chairman of the National Arts Council of Zimbabwe, John Mapondera, was convinced it could happen. The support and great organisational skills of Roy and Meg Guthrie from Gallery Shona Sculpture and Chapungu Village in Harare ensured that over thirty-five tons of stone carving were crated and transported by sea, air, road and rail to Yorkshire in time for the opening. Their assistance has been crucial. I am also grateful to them for the loan of many significant sculptures, as I am to Mr & Mrs Roy Cooke of Matombo Gallery in Harare, who apart from lending important sculptures have been supportive from the outset. I was also delighted to be able to borrow works from the National Gallery of Zimbabwe and appreciate the help of the Director, Professor Rogers and his staff for their cooperation and advice.

The political and financial support of the government of Zimbabwe has been critical. Apart from the generous financial contribution made by the National Arts Council of Zimbabwe; along with the enthusiastic support of Fay Chung, the Minister of Education and Culture; the significance of the event was forcefully underlined when Dr Joshua Nkomo, Honourable Senior Minister and Vice President of Zimbabwe, visited the Yorkshire Sculpture Park to open the exhibition on Saturday 21 July 1990. This great gesture will long be cherished by the artists of Zimbabwe, the Yorkshire Sculpture Park and the crowds who greeted Dr Nkomo at the opening ceremony.

While mentioning the support from Zimbabwe I cannot overlook the work of the staff of the National Arts Council, in particular Kate Chifamba, who was also present at the opening. Still in Zimbabwe I was appreciative of the staff of the British Council in Harare who worked wonders on our behalf, particulary Shoba Ponappa, meticulously dealing with many telephone calls and distributing

Dr Joshua Nkomo
at the opening of the exhibition

INTRODUCTION

Extracts from the address by Dr Joshua Nkomo on the occasion of the opening of the exhibition, 21 July 1990

This exhibition of Zimbabwe Stone Sculpture is part of a year long programme of events to celebrate the Tenth Independence Anniversary of Zimbabwe, the Zimbabwe festival - *Zimfest 1990* which has been planned by the National Arts Council of Zimbabwe whose Chairman, John Mapondera, is here in Yorkshire as part of the Zimbabwean contingent. The exhibition was organised by the Yorkshire Sculpture Park, with the support of the National Arts Council of Zimbabwe, the National Gallery of Zimbabwe, the Gallery Shona Sculpture, Matombo Gallery, other private galleries in Harare all working in harmonious relationship.

We also celebrate here the highest achievements of Zimbabwean artists who over the years have struggled to attain skills without any formal training. The former director of the National Gallery of Zimbabwe, Frank McEwen, singularly gave a new impetus to stone sculpture in Zimbabwe in the early Sixties. Since then many other promoters of this unique art have also played a part. The Zimbabwe Government acknowledges these important contributions and this exhibition provides an opportunity to judge critically what has been achieved. It affords the international community and art critics the opportunity to evaluate the true worth of the stone sculpture of Zimbabwe.

From where I stand, as one of the leaders of a country with which the United Kingdom enjoys a special relationship, this exhibition serves to underline that cooperation. Sadly, there is a tendency to view cultural exchanges as a secondary priority in our cooperation not only with the United Kingdom but also with the European Community as a whole. It is unfortunate that too often attention is concentrated on trade and diplomatic cooperation, while the field of culture, which has a very important role to play in enriching and providing depth in our historical ties, is overlooked.

In all countries myth has an historical, cultural and social significance. A belief in myth can, in a sense, be equated with faith which is essentially a belief in the intangible and what cannot be proven. Myth is articulated in Africa mainly through folk-lore which can provide a cosmological rationale for a world view which is believed, but which cannot be subjected to scientific proof. Myth plays an important part in the life of all people and in Africa it provides the link between the mortal and invisible worlds, the living and the dead, the visible and the invisible universe.

The apogee of Zimbabwean civilisation, Great Zimbabwe, which dates from about 1250 to 1450 AD, was until recently shrouded in myth and conjecture. According to legend, which itself was underpinned by the colonial settlement of the country, Great Zimbabwe was settled by the European, Egyptians, the Phoneacians and even Martians.

Today, archaeologicial research has established that Great Zimbabwe was a settlement of the Shona, the name now given to the people who settled on the high plateau of the country around 900AD. The now ruined settlement, preceded by a settlement of a less grand scale, Mapungubwe, and succeeded by others - for example Ruzwi around Bulawayo (1450 - 1650), Mutapa (1490 - 1650), and Changamire (1690 - 1800) - still speaks eloquently of the people, their social organisation, their aesthetic sophistication and their domestic skills. The famed Zimbabwe stone birds, six of which were discovered in the eastern enclosure of Great Zimbabwe thought to be the home of

Damian Manuhwa
Mother and Child 1989

Henry Munyaradzi
Fish Eagle Watching 1985

have an effect on the weather. Stone itself has geological significance, and this is important to the sculptors. Within an indoor gallery, these sculptures take on an appearance far removed from the intentions of the artists. In a gallery space, the sculptures' cultural significance is subdued by the fact that they become 'art objects', denuded of their proper meaning. In this outdoor setting, the monumentality of the works of John and Bernard Takawira and Nicholas Mukomberanwa will be seen in its own right. Space is an important word for sculpture, not just space which can be seen within but the surrounding space.

Here in the Yorkshire Sculpture Park the epic sweep of the work of the late John Takawira is apparent in its true poetic sense, as is the geological form of the stone. Here the hard edged lines and angular and severe forms of the recent work of Nicholas Mukomberanwa are softened by the natural setting of the work. Here the works of Bernard Takawira, stone ravaged by space, rest easily, as they would in the grounds of his farm at Bromley, outside Harare.

Like Brancusi, like Michelangelo, and like Moore, the sculptors of Zimbabwe have established their own direction, but without formal art education. For Zimbabwean sculptors, like their Western predecessors, the life force of their work is born both from within their materials and from within themselves. Joram Mariga, through the encouragement of his nephew, the late John Takawira, Moses Masaya, Crispen Chakabnyuka and many others, developed in Zimbabwean sculpture a unique appreciation of the natural qualities of stone.

There are many individuals and organisations whose support has made this exhibition possible, most of them are appropriately acknowledged in the catalogue. Allow me to add the Government of Zimbabwe's sincere appreciation of their support and the personal congratulations of myself and of his Excellency the President of the Republic of Zimbabwe, Comrade Robert Mugabe, for the magnificent display realised here at the Yorkshire Sculpture Park.

Joshua Nkomo was born on 7 June 1917, in the Kezi area of Zimbabwe. His political life started with the Rhodesian African Workers Union. He became the first President of the African National Congress (ANC) in 1957 and in 1961 the President of the Zimbabwean African People's Union (ZAPU). After imprisonment in 1963 and ten years banishment in 1964 for involvement in the national liberation movement he fought for Independence through both negotiation and the armed struggle. He was Commander-in-Chief of the Zimbabwe Peoples Revolutionary Army (ZIPRA) and joint leader of the Patriotic Front which negiotiated the Lancaster House Agreement for the Independence of Zimbabwe. Currently Senior Minister in the Office of the President and Cabinet and responsible for Development, he is also Vice President of the ruling ZANU PF and Vice President of the Republic of Zimbabwe.

Opposite:

Bernard Takawira
At One with my Spirit 1988

CONTEMPORARY STONE CARVING FROM ZIMBABWE

Michael Shepherd

Really the person who should be writing this introduction to the contemporary stone carving of Zimbabwe is Frank McEwen - who by the grace of God is still alive to tell the tale; and every teacher and administrator who hopes to draw the miracle of art out of the deep dark of the unmanifest should sit at his feet and hear it.

It is not only a story of profound general truth; historically, it is one of the rare golden deeds of late colonialism - or indeed, post-colonialism; since although the story begins in the late 1950s, we have Frank's word for it that not a single influential white person in Rhodesia took any interest in this great adventure of art in its early days.

Sylvester Mubayi
Spirit of the Mountain 1990

It was an adventure in spirit which needed the equal participation of two parties: human beings who were drawn to find form for their own soul, and the soul of their tribe or nation, by carving stone; and someone who could help to draw that out of them - purely. Perhaps only Carl Jung could do justice to this story of personal voyages into the collective mind and imagination.

Frank McEwen had grown up with his father's collection of African art; and had sat at the feet of Henry Focillon in Paris around 1926: Focillon, "a loving understander" of all forms of great art that spring from spirit, and a close admirer of the teachings of Gustave Moreau, which were designed to draw art out of human beings which was true to their individual self. And as the Fine Arts representative of the British Council in Paris, Frank McEwen introduced Henry Moore to the French in 1945, culminating in his first Paris exhibition in 1945: an appropriate connection with the venue of this exhibition in Yorkshire where Moore, Hepworth and others re-introduced direct carving of stone to British contemporary art in the 1930s.

So when McEwen was first contacted in 1954 about the building of a proposed National Gallery of Southern Rhodesia regarding architecture, a permanent collection and a dynamic purpose for the gallery, not only dependent on borrowing art from abroad, he was well prepared for this adventure (though the museum itself was intended for non-African art); and when he was appointed its first Director, the adventure began - slowly. While the foundations were still going up, Frank and Thomas Mukarobgwa sat on the low walls every day and Thomas told Frank about the Shona people, their religion, their dance, and their music. And when the gallery was built, it was a year after Frank had slowly infiltrated potential artists into the security and curatorial staff, and given them crayons and paint, that the urge to carve and sculpt - long forgotten in Zimbabwe and virtually without surviving traces - emerged again spontaneously, without his planning it.

Nicholas Mukomberanwa
The Corrupting Power of Money 1985

PERSONAL REFLECTIONS

Frank McEwen

In writing for this publication I find myself in the curious position of the old man leaning on his gate in the sunshine asking passers-by "Who's out? Who's in?" and wondering if the vitality and purity of this work in its initial phase in the late 1950s to early 1970s can be protected in the face of explosive development.

Sir Laurence van der Post, with a deep understanding of the African dilemma, has spoken of the "profound and unspoken religious hunger in man" and the "reawakening of the importance of the natural world".

In their sculpture the artists of Zimbabwe have given us, carved directly in rough hard stone, symbols of this spiritual hunger with superb untutored craftsmanship. Such is their skill that they rarely make a mistake in execution or depart from their inner vision.

They have anticipated the estrangement from the environment in the mythological themes evident today, which are derided by some as 'ethnic' and which are nevertheless eternal symbols found in all great cultures of the world and which relate directly back to the idea of the collective unconscious of Carl Jung.

How did this expression through sculpture come into being as if it were from nowhere? I believe it was a rare combination of a vital and unspoilt people with a profound but destabilised ancient artistic background dating back three hundred years to the stone carvings of birds and winged figures now in the Tishman collection and the protection of a recently created National Gallery with a dynamic concept of art and no art school mentality.

Sylvester Mubayi
Mudzimu (Spirit) Bull 1978

Thomas Mukarobgwa
Be Still my Child 1983

To quote Pierre Descargues of France Culture - "It was as if the Shona sculptors had taken up their tools where their Zimbabwe ancestors had laid them down... was not art a forerunner of Independence?"

I had hardly heard of Rhodesia when nearly 40 years ago in Paris I wrote an introduction for another exhibition "Young Artists: École de Paris". It was widely criticised, as for me a new wave of 'Trivialism' was overtaking the world centre of creative art. "If some vital new art exists or is about to exist ... it may occur elsewhere, in a different walk of life with a different raison d'être: prompted by a new environment".

Although the School of Paris had been revitalised by new images essentially from Africa, and "Les Demoiselles des bords de la Seine" had become " Les Demoiselles D'Avignon", already by 1950 some deeper-thinking people were aware of the decline of the International School of Paris. Though the giants of the Brancusi, Leger, Picasso generation were still in place, the attics of France were now overflowing with multi-coloured triangles, as in the 1920s Monet's retreat in Giverny had been totally surrounded by earnest easels. It became necessary to find a new beginning.

Having in a pre-war experiment guided a creative workshop in Toulon based on the principles of Gustave Moreau I took, in 1954, on Herbert Read's advice, the first position of adviser on the creation of a new museum in Africa (a building, a collection and a creative aim). From 1955 I then held the position of the first director of the National

Following page:

Joram Mariga
Spirit of Zimbabwe 1989

Edward Masaya
Spiritual Construction 1988

Samson Kuvhengurwa
Bushman Thinking 1989

Joseph Muzondo
Bringing the Sad News 1990

Previous page:

Agnes Nyanhongo
Zimbabwe Bird 1990

Albert Mamvura
Spirit Protecting Chief 1990

Gallery of Rhodesia, now Zimbabwe. There had been the necessary time at sea to reflect upon the mission and a method, as I had been for thirteen months under sail from Paris to Mozambique via Brazil and Cape Town.

From the liberal atmosphere of France I found myself in a stifling colony. My early efforts at encouraging art in every section of the community were met with hostility and total misunderstanding. The only art to be found was airport art, mass-produced tourist souvenirs sold on the streets.

Beginning in 1956, I was inspired by the unlimited explosion of talent evident in the work produced at first by the Museum staff using painting materials and then stone. Later, with numbers of would-be artists from all over the country coming and going freely in the informal gallery workshop, the movement had begun.

Support and recognition of the quality of the work (both painting and sculpture) came from European and American museum directors, collectors and experts, among them Alfred Barr, Tristan Tzara and Roland Penrose. They gave the necessary authentication and after a year of struggle our free-lance workshop with its spirit of freedom became part of the National Gallery.

As individual artists developed, their work inexplicably reflected various phases of artistic expression from 'pre-Columbian', 'Ancient Egyptian' stone power to spiritual Surrealism. Inexplicable because there was *no* exterior influence, only instinct from within.

In spite of our success abroad with the Museum of Modern Art in New York in 1968, the Musée Rodin in Paris 1971 and the ICA in London in 1972, tension in Rhodesia became such that I resigned in 1973.

After a break due to the hostilities in 1980 development is again advancing with outstanding results both technically and sculpturally. Perhaps one day some of the sculptures may be compared with those of antiquity, with genius of form that reveals eternal meaning.

Now there are new, vital and articulate young artists of integrity following the 'tradition' started by the first great masters; John and Bernard Takawira, Mukomberanwa, Mubayi, Ndandarika, Mariga, Matemera, and Henry and Thomas Mukarobgwa, the very first member of the workshop. These were all present in the 1971 Musée Rodin exhibition.

But who are the protectors and supporters of new art? There are no longer ancient potentates and Pharaohs. Museums rarely if ever promote living but as yet unknown people. In recent times only those rare great dealers as opposed to the marketeering ones fight against all odds for a cause, such as the Durand Ruell brothers for the Impressionists at the turn of the century or the great Daniel Henri Kahnweiler before and after the two world wars for the School of

Henry Munyaradzi
The Good Shepherd 1989

Joseph Ndandarika
After the Struggle 1990

Paris. I have always believed inspired dealers have this main challenge to fulfil.

As the old man who once encouraged and tried to protect this new flowering of creativity when it was not fashionable to do so in the climate of Rhodesian intolerance, I watch with excitement and curiosity the growing consciousness of the new wave of free young artists. If it remains a truly contemporary force but combines also successfully with the ancient cultural heritage of the great people of Zimbabwe it may help to give the 21st century the inspiration it so urgently requires.

Here is a hopeful note of promise and encouragement.

Reproduced by kind permission of Felicity Wright and Gimpel Fils.

Frank McEwen, OBE, lived in France before the last war for fourteen years, which included two years study of the History of Art with Henri Focillon. From 1945 he was for a decade the fine arts representative of the British Council in Paris.

After an initial trip to Zimbabwe, then Rhodesia in 1954 to help plan the National Art Gallery, he became the founding director in 1956, a post he held until his resignation in 1973. From 1959 he lectured widely in the USA.

Joseph Ndandarika
After the Struggle 1990

Previous pages:

Joseph Ndandarika
Farmer Resting 1983

Bernard Matemera
Chapungu 1985

These pages:

Bernard Matemera
Blind Man 1988

John Takawira
Chapungu Landing 1987

Tapfuma Gutsa
Lessons from the San People 1987

Following pages:

Tapfuma Gutsa
Listening to the Baby Kick 1988

Henry Munyaradzi
Saviour and Child 1989

Tapfuma Gutsa
The Galaxy (unfinished)

These pages:

Bernard Takawira
The Power of Humility 1988

John Takawira
The Lovers 1988

Boira Mteki
Protecting the Twins 1972

Following pages:

Enos Gunja
Bird Resting 1969/70

Simon Machile
Elephant 1969

COMMUNICATING WITH THE EARTH SPIRIT

Statement by Joram Mariga

The following extract is edited from an interview conducted with Joram Mariga when he worked at the YSP (along with fellow artists Bernard Takawira and Tapfuma Gutsa) from 22 - 30 July 1990

I started as a sculptor when I was a little boy of eight or nine, carving in wood. I was a herdboy and made some images of cattle, learning from my father and brothers about how they used to carve. When I had qualified as an agriculturalist and was working in Nyanga some tractors grading a road turned up a piece of soapstone, greenish in colour and about the size of a peach seed. I scratched away at this soap-like piece and then decided to find out where it came from. I roamed around and found the source, took away a bigger piece and started to carve stone for the first time; little things to please myself. After five years carving I came across Mrs Pearce who introduced me to Frank McEwen.

Most of the sculptors today are carving in serpentine but I have gone a little bit ahead and I am using lepidolite. This is the rock that I used for the sculpture I call *"Spirit of Zimbabwe"* (page 28); if you look carefully at this stone it contains three colours, lilac purple, darker purple and grey. The name was suggested by someone else and I am content with it, the three colours to me suggest deeper thinking about what is happening in Zimbabwe.

The sculpture, *"Communicating with the Earth Spirit"*, began when I bought the stone. It took me quite some time before I started work on it because sometimes an idea runs away from my mind and also because this piece is so big it needs six people to struggle to move it. I'm hoping to buy a block and tackle to move some large blocks because I am worried that one day someone else will be crushed by a big piece of stone. When I was finishing carving the piece I found I had made what I call a "crime" because I didn't know how to carve

Joram Mariga
Communicating with the Earth Spirit 1990

the type of pattern, the faint lines, which are on the face of the sculpture. At a later stage I became aware of the way I was holding the chisel and found that if I held it loosely it was possible to make those lines. I realised when I had finished that the sculpture is divided into two divisions, the head from above the chest I wanted polished. I called the sculpture "Kutauriran" which means "talking together".

In our own custom we believe that there is a connection between the dead and the living. The white side of "Kutauriran" represents the living, the polished portion which is a little bit darker represents the spirits which are the dead ancestors. The sculpture also shows that a human being should be aware of the surroundings he lives in. The faint little lines represent sheet erosion which means that when rain is falling and wind blowing the human must be careful, otherwise he cannot be aware of the condition of his surroundings. The contours show that if a person is aware he can stop the top soil from being washed away, he can build contours so that he will be able to live for a long time.

Following page:

Joram Mariga
Communicating with the Earth Spirit 1990

Gladman Zinyeka
Mukadzi 1990

Bernard Matemera
Hippo Boy 1986

Damian Manuhwa
Arms Control 1990

Boira Mteki
Beer for the Spirits 1987

STONES OF ZIMBABWE

The following notes provide brief background information on some of the stones used by the sculptors of Zimbabwe. They have been compiled with the help of Bernard Takawira and Roy Guthrie.

SERPENTINE

Serpentine is found in many deposits throughout Zimbabwe and its colour varies between brown, green, red, orange, mauve, varigated and black. The green, brown and black varieties are found at Tengenenge. The exceptionally hard black serpentine variety is known as "Springstone". The best of these Tengenenge Serpentines have a fine texture with no cleavages, are hard and firm so offer a good resistance to the sculptor, and are wrapped in the outer "blanket" of reddish brown oxidised rock. They emerge from the quarry like sculptures created by nature millions of years ago and are often a source of inspiration to the artist.

RED SERPENTINE

Found in Guruve, it can range in hardness from very soft to unworkable. Naturally formed in varigated bands of red, green, mauve, and black.

OTHER SERPENTINES

Red, mauve, brown etc found all over Zimbabwe and used by artists when good quality is available.

STEATITE

The Masano deposit at Tengenenge provides very beautiful red, green, brown, orange and pink steatites. It is a softer stone than serpentine.

VERDITE

A rare semi-precious green stone found only in two locations world-wide. The Zimbabwe deposit is considered to be of particularly high

Saidi Sabiti
Twins 1986

quality because of its hardness and beautiful variations of colour. It is known as Ruby Verdite, because of the presence of corundum in much of the stone.

GOLDEN VERDITE

A variety of verdite lacking the presence of chrome which gives verdite its green colour. The result is a rich gold brown stone normally softer than green verdite (but even more rare).

LEOPARD ROCK

A rarely used ornamental stone found in the Nyanga area. Very hard and characterised by blotches of yellow and black; hence the name "Leopard Rock".

SIPOLILO STONE

A very hard orange/yellow serpentine found in the Guruve area (formerly Sipolilo).

LIMESTONE

Close to the capital city, Harare, is found a hard, finely grained grey limestone deposit.

MARBLE

Zimbabwe has vast deposits of white, grey and varigated marbles.

Henry Munyaradzi
Spirit Lion 1986

Ephraim Chaurika
Horse 1988

Bernard Matemera
Elephant Man 1987

ARTISTS: BIOGRAPHICAL NOTES

Fanizani Akuda
I know you have stolen my eggs 1988

Ephraim Chaurika
Horse 1988

Samwell Chirume
Baboon Babysitter 1988

FANIZANI AKUDA

Born in 1932 in Zambia of the Chewwa Tribe. Akuda's family came to Zimbabwe in 1949 and he was first introduced to sculpture when he was employed by the sculptors at Tengenenge to dig stone. Since then he has become an active member of the Tengenenge Sculpture Community.

Known professionally as Fanizani, his distinctive style of curved and rounded forms are inspired by human and animal forms which are often intermixed. He has participated in all the important group exhibitions and has work in many collections.

EPHRAIM CHAURIKA

Born in Guruve. After school Chaurika's first job was as a watch repairer. He was an early member of the Tengenenge Sculpture Community but he now lives and works in Harare. His early work reflected much mysticism but in recent years his work has become more decorative. He is a technically skilful artist who derives his inspiration from nature. Chaurika has participated in all the Tengenenge group exhibitions and has work in many collections including the Volkerkunde Museum, Frankfurt, Germany.

SAMWELL CHIRUME

Born circa 1940. Did not start making sculpture until late in life and is a recent arrival at the Sculptors Community of Tengenenge where he has established a firm friendship with Bernard Matemera. This productive relationship has enabled Chirume, along with Matemera, to produce some of the most powerful and original work to come out of Tengengenge. Recently he has has exhibited regularly and won several awards including, in 1988, first prize in the National Art Gallery Nedlaw exhibition.

Enos Gunja
Bird Resting 1969/70

Tapfuma Gutsa
Antelope changing into Bird 1988

Paul Gwichiri
Man changing into Bird 1989

Makina Kameya
Angola Girl 1985

ENOS GUNJA

Born in Guruve in 1946 and known as *"Gunja"*. Gunja was one of the founder members of the Tengenenge Sculpture Community. He is also a good friend of the sculptor Chaurika who he worked with for many years. Although he has exhibited extensively and has work in important collections he is not at present actively engaged in making sculpture.

TAPFUMA GUTSA

Born in 1956 in Harare. Educated at St Ignatius College, Chishawasha. After working for his father's construction company he started wood carving under Cornelius Manguma at Driefontein Mission, Mvuma from 1978-1979. Later he was awarded a British Council scholarship to study sculpture at the City and Guilds School of Art, Londo (1982-85).

Gutsa carves in stone and wood and often combines both in his sculptures. He is constantly experimenting and extending his vocabulary as an artist. He has a deep empathy and concern for people and social concerns which are often reflected in his sensitive handling of the subject matter and material. Exhibited extensively in Zimbabe, Britain and other parts of Europe and has work in many private and public collections.

PAUL GWICHIRI

Born in Nyanga in 1938. Gwichiri came to Harare in 1957 and joined the staff of the National Gallery in 1962 where he has worked ever since as an attendant. He started to make sculpture in 1964 when he became a member of the Workshop School at the National Gallery. He has exhibited extensively nationally and also in London and Paris. His work can be seen in private and public collections including the National Gallery of Zimbabwe, the Gallery Shona Sculpture and Chapungu Village in Harare.

MAKINA KAMEYA

Born in 1918 in Angola. As a youth his grandfather taught him to carve wooden dishes from which he made a small income. After working on his parents' farm he moved to Zimbabwe in 1945 obtaining work as a gardener. Later he worked as a chrome miner and also as an agricultural labourer. In 1958 Kameya moved to Tengenenge and when the Sculpture Community started in 1966 he started to make sculpture.

His sculpture reflects the influence of West African masks and apart from human spirit forms he also sculpts birds. Late in life he achieved recognition and won major awards at the National Gallery. Sadly Kameya died tragically in 1987 when a large sculpture he was working on at Tengenenge fell on top of him.

Samson Kuvhengurwa
Moon Man 1989

Simon Machile
Elephant 1969

Wazi Maicolo

Albert Mamvura
Spirit of Wisdom 1990

SAMSON KUVHENGURWA

Born in 1953 at Muchinyo Village in the Mudzi area of Mutoko. Kuvhengurwa comes from an artistic family. His father was headman of his village and was also a farmer and carver of traditional artifacts. His mother worked with clay, making pots and his four brothers are also sculptors. As a child he made baskets, carved walking sticks and African plates to assist with the family income. His grandfather was a famous carver of traditional musical instruments and drums and was a sense of inspiration to all the family.

After school he worked as labourer, hotel waiter and travelling salesman before he joined Canon Paterson as a soapstone carver and went on to supply Gallery Africa with his work. Returning to Mutoko he started to carve large wood carvings and won an award in the 1982 Nedlaw exhibition. Following this he worked in Botswana using goldstone. He is often known as Sam Kuvhe which is how he signs his works and has work in many collections including the Botswana National Gallery.

SIMON MACHILE

Although little documentation exists it is known that Simon was born in Angola and in his youth learnt to carve traditional Mikishi masks and wooden figures used for ritual purposes. He came to Zimbabwe to work in the chromium mines and joined the Tengenenge Sculpture Community in 1966 and was an active member of the group until his death in 1977. Few of Simon's sculptures remain in Zimbabwe. However, a group of his works were found recently in South Africa by Gallery Shona Sculpture and returned to Zimbabwe where they have been exhibited ever since. As an artist he was known as *Simon* and often signed his work *Saimon*.

WAZI MAICOLO

Born in Angola circa 1926. As the cook for the manager of a farm near Tengenenge he joined the Tengenenge Sculptors Community working there in his spare time. Virtually until his death in 1986 he produced powerful and original sculpture. The National Gallery honoured his memory with a retrospective of his sculpture and subsequently acquired most of his work for their permanent collection.

ALBERT MAMVURA

Born in 1954 in the Buhera District Mamvura grew up in a rural environment. After leaving school he qualified as a carpenter and worked for several construction companies. He was introduced to sculpture by his cousin Nicholas Mukomberanwa. In 1977 Mamvura started to work as a sculptor on his own. His work is inspired by studies of both people and nature and often reflect the loose knit family relationship of Shona society. He has exhibited frequently and has works in private and public collections including those of the Botswana National Museum, Queen Sofia of Spain and Prince Charles.

Damian Manuhwa
Musikana (Young Girl) 1989

Bernard Manyandure
Antelope in a Trance

Josiah Manzi
Hippo Man 1976

Joram Mariga
Communicating with the Earth Spirit 1990

DAMIAN MANUHWA

Born in 1952 at Tanda Communal Area of Rusape District and educated at St Michael's School, Headlands. In 1969 Manuhwa started to make sculpture and joined the National Gallery Workshop School until 1971. In 1973 he became a bus driver and carved in his spare time. In 1980 he became a full time artist and continues to work successfully today. He has participated in major exhibitions since 1970 and has work in important collections.

BERNARD MANYANDURE

Born in 1952 at Nyatate in Nyanga North. Manyandure, along with a number of other sculptors, formed the Nyanga group under the leadership of Joram Mariga where he met Frank McEwen who gave further encouragement. Although he has exhibited extensively and has work in several collections most of his time is now taken up with his farm in Nyanga, making sculpture in his spare time.

JOSIAH MANZI

Born in Zimbabwe of Malawian parents, Manzi worked as a labourer on a tobacco farm before joining the Tengenenge Sculpture Community in 1966 where he still works. An important member of the group his subject matter is influenced by the natural and spiritual world. He has exhibited in all important group exhibitions.

JORAM MARIGA

Born in 1927 near Chinoye in Zimbabwe. As a child Mariga observed his father and brother carve wood for pleasure and his mother make open-fired ceramics. He started wood carving at the age of nine and at school he joined the wood working class. In later life he taught wood carving to family and friends including his nephew John Takawira.

Mariga became one of the founder members of the Nyanga group. He is reputed to be the first artist to start carving soapstone in Zimbabwe and is considered by many to be the father of Shona sculpture. An influential and inspirational figure in the development of stone sculpture in Zimbabwe he has taught and encouraged many to start making sculpture. He has exhibited extensively since 1962 and participated in all the major group exhibitions.

EDWARD TENDAYI MASAYA

Born in 1960 in Nyanga. After schooling Masaya went to college for two years. In 1980 he worked under his cousin Moses Masaya and in 1982 he worked for a short period with Brighton Sango in Guruve. Masaya is a great admirer of Nicholas Mukomberanwa and Joseph Ndandarika. Since 1980 he has participated in many exhibitions in Zimbabwe and other countries.

Edward Masaya
Spiritual Construction 1988

Moses Masaya
Spirited Magician 1990

Mike Masedza
Mastermind 1989

Bernard Matemera
Possessed by Woman 1988

MOSES MASAYA

Born in 1947 in Nyanga. After working under Joram Mariga in 1967 Masaya established and directed the Village Art and Craft Centre in Nyanga which became a show place for his and other artists' work. Throughout this period he was encouraged by Frank McEwen who bought work for the permanent collection at the National Gallery. His preference is for the green, goldstone and black serpentine stone of his home lands in Nyanga. Participated in all major group exhibitions including the important exhibition held at the Musée Rodin, Paris in 1971.

MIKE MASEDZA

Born in 1967, four years after the declaration of UDI Masedza grew up during the struggle for Independence. He lived in the Makori district in the eastern Highlands with his grandparents until the age of seven and spent his time herding cattle, collecting firewood and listening to his 'grandfather's wisdom'. He organized his own secondary education which he completed after Independence in 1980. At sixteen years of age he joined Joseph Ndandarika and worked with him for five years. Since 1983 he has exhibited regularly and participated in exhibitions in Zimbabwe, Canada, Australia, New York, London and Glasgow.

BERNARD MATEMERA

Born in 1946 in Guruve. At school Matemera excelled at wood carving and in his youth as a cattle herder he made clay figures. An early member of the Tengengene Sculpture Community he was one of the few artists who remained there during the war of independence. He continues to live and work there. His work is uncompromisingly African and his subjects are derived from people, animals and dreams. Matemera has exhibited extensively and recently received a major award at the New Delhi Triennale and he has also won first prize in the Nedlaw Sculpture Competition at the National Gallery of Zimbabwe. His work can be seen in many important collections throughout the world.

BOIRA MTEKI

Born in 1946 in Harare. After working at Nyarutsetse Art Centre under Canon Paterson, Boira Mteki joined the workshop at the National Gallery under the direction of Frank McEwen.

Boira Mteki was an important and major force in the early development of stone carving in Zimbabwe. However, due to lack of support he started to make soapstone curios to survive. More recently he has received greater recognition and support and is at present at the Gallery Shona Sculpture, Chapungu village, working on a large sculpture from a ten ton block of limestone for the National Gallery. His preference is for hard stone, particularly limestones. Promoted and supported for many years by the Gallery Shona Sculpture he has work in many collections and participated in all of the early group exhibitions.

RICHARD MTEKI

Born in Harare in 1947. Richard Mteki's father was a mechanic and his brother Boira Mteki is an important sculptor in Zimbabwe. After primary school he joined the Nyarutsetse Art Centre established by Canon Paterson.

Following this he joined the National Gallery Workshop and received the encouragement of Frank McEwen. He left in 1973 and since then has worked independently. His preferred stone is brown serpentine and his preferred subject matter the human form. In 1982 President Mugabe presented a sculpture by Mteki to the President of Nigeria and his work can also be seen in many other collections. He has exhibited extensively since 1969 in Zimbabwe, Europe, North America and Australia.

SYLVESTER MUBAYI

Born in 1942 in the Chiota Reserve, near Marondera. After leaving school Mubayi worked as a tobacco grader and moved to Harare in 1966 to seek employment at the Chibuku Breweries. In 1967 he jointed the Sculptors Community at Tengenenge. Later he was a founder member of the Vukutu Workshop School established by Frank McEwen who much later in 1987 said of him "Certainly when I knew him he was by far the greatest sculptor there ... I have tremendeous admiration for him ... some of his work is as great as anything in the world."

Mubayi now lives and works in Chitunguiza. His work is inspired by a world of spirit and supernatural forces often fusing people and the animal world. His early work was inspired by skeletons. He has exhibited extensively since 1968 in many parts of the world and has work in major collections in Europe and North America.

THOMAS MUKAROBGWA

Born in Rusape in 1924. Mukarobgwa joined the staff of the National Gallery of Zimbabwe in 1957 where he still works as an attendant. Originally a painter it was thanks to Frank McEwen's encouragement that Thomas Moo, as he is called, began to make sculpture. He was the winner of the Nedlaw Sculpture Exhibition in 1982 and he has exhibited extensively in Zimbabwe, London, Paris, New York and Australia. His work can be seen in many private and public collections including the National Gallery of Zimbabwe, the Museum of Modern Art, New York and The Gallery Shona Sculpture, Chapungu Village in Harare.

Boira Mteki
Ambuyia 1972

Richard Mteki
Owl Protecting Family 1986

Sylvester Mubayi
Warrior Whistling 1990

Thomas Mukarobgwa
I hope you are a good spirit 1983

Nicholas Mukomberanwa
The Greedy One 1985

Henry Munyaradzi
Swallow 1989

Joseph Muzondo
Desperate Mother 1990

Joseph Muzondo
Bringing the Sad News 1990

NICHOLAS MUKOMBERANWA

Born in 1940 in the Buhera District near Rusape, Mukomberanwa attended Serima Mission and started wood carving under the direction of Father Groeber. In 1961 he moved to Harare and joined the Police force. After meeting Frank McEwen he became a member of the National Gallery Workshop and was also a part-time member of the Vukutu Workshop. In 1976 he left the police to become a full time sculptor. He now lives and works on his farm near to Harare.

Mukomberanwa has exhibited extensively throughout Africa, Europe and North America and is considered to be one of the most important sculptors working in Zimbabwe. His work can be seen in many important collections including the National Gallery of Zimbabwe, the National Gallery of Botswana, the Field Museum Chicago, the Museum of Mankind, London and the Volkerkunde Museum, Frankfurt.

HENRY MUNYARADZI

Born in Guruve in 1931. Munyaradzi's father was a spirit medium who left the family when Munyaradzi was one year old and never returned. As a result, Munyaradzi was brought up by an uncle in a rural environment and had no formal schooling. After working for the village blacksmith he then worked on tobacco farms as a carpenter and tobacco grader. In 1967, out of work, he discovered Tengenenge, a sculptors' community established by Tom Blomefield, an ex tobacco farmer. In Tengenenge Henry Munyaradzi started to make sculpture and he soon established himself as an important member of the group. Ever since his first exhibition at the National Gallery of Zimbabwe in 1968 he has exhibited extensively both nationally and internationally. He now owns a farm in Zimbabwe where he lives and works, continuing to be inspired by the rural setting and the shape of the stones he carves.

JOSEPH MUZONDO

Born in 1953, Muzondo joined a National Gallery Workshop as a student in 1981. He is an artist in the widest sense and has worked as a textile designer in Tanzania as well as studying etching and engraving techniques in Europe.

Muzondo's work has been exhibited internationally and he has had the unusual honour of having a piece chosen to illustrate some Zimbabwean postage stamps. His work appears in both the permanent and overseas collections of the National Gallery of Zimbabwe.

AMON MWAREKA

Born in Nyanga in 1950. In 1969 he met Frank McEwen and became an active member of the Vukutu Workshop which had been started by Frank McEwen. He now lives in Harare where he continues to

Joseph Ndandarika
Togetherness 1982

Agnes Nyanhongo
Water Spirit 1990

Agnes Nyanhongo
Zimbabwe Bird 1990

Saidi Sabiti
Eagle Man 1987

make sculpture. He has exhibited extensively nationally and also in Paris and London. He has work in several collections including the National Gallery of Zimbabwe and the Gallery Shona Sculpture, Chapungu Village in Harare.

JOSEPH NDANDARIKA

Born in 1940 in Harare he grew up near Mutare. His grandfather was a well known witch doctor and as a youth he was apprenticed to a N'Anga (witch doctor). Later he was educated at Serima Mission School where he was converted to Catholicism and started to paint, draw and carve.

Ndandarika was one of the earliest members of the workshop school established at the National Gallery by Frank McEwen. Although his first love is sculpture Ndandarika is also a gifted painter and the Museum of Modern Art in New York purchased one of his earliest paintings. Steeped in traditional Shona custom and folk-lore he draws heavily on this background as an inspiration for his work. Frank McEwen has described Ndandarika as a universal genius who has worked in every possible medium. He has been a leading figure in the development of contemporary sculpture in Zimbabwe since the mid 1960s. Ndandarika has exhibited extensively both nationally and internationally and has work in major private and public collections throughout the world. One of Zimbabwe's major sculptors, he was recently honoured by the country through the issue of a set of commemorative stamps depicting his work.

AGNES NYANHONGO

Born in 1960 in Nyanga. Nyanhongo's father, Claud, is a well known sculptor. After leaving school she started work as a shop assistant before starting to make in sculpture in 1987. As a child she helped her father and in 1984 she joined the BAT workshops for three years.

Agnes Nyanhongo is married to the sculptor Joseph Munemo. She is an active member of ZIIA, an organisation devoted to the support of the physically and mentally handicapped. Her work has been shown on a regular basis in Zimbabwe and has been included in a number of international exhibitions.

SAIDI SABITI

Born in Mozambique in 1929, Sabiti came to Zimbabwe in 1949 to work in the mines and on farms. He has had no formal schooling or education. Sabiti started carving wood and in 1966 joined the Tengenenge Sculptor Community and has since worked in stone.

His subjects range from delicate birds to images of powerful water spirits and mystic metamorphic creatures. Often carves on a large scale and it is reputed that his *Sitting Chief* made in black serpentine is the largest carving to be made in Zimbabwe. At present he works at the Chapungu Sculpture Garden in Harare. He has exhibited extensively and has work in important collections.

Brighton Sango
Woman Kneeling & Prayer for us All 1988

BRIGHTON SANGO

Born in 1958 in Guruve. Coming from a poor family Sango's formal education ended at an early age. After short contact with the Tengenenge Sculpture Community he started to work on his own and like most other sculptors from Zimbabwe is self taught. In 1989 he moved to Harare where he continues to work. As part of the second generation of artists from Zimbabwe, Sango's work is not as influenced by Shona culture and tradition as others. Nor is it influenced by cubism which the artist has no knowledge of. His inspiration comes from within and is based upon his personal interpretation of nature - the light, shadows and images which surround him. He has exhibited regularly since 1981 in Zimbabwe, London, Germany, North America, Ireland and Hong Kong.

Norbert Shamuyarira
The Shame of being Me 1986

NORBERT SHAMUYARIRA

Born in 1962 in Chinhoyi, Mashonaland. Shamuyarira started to make sculpture in 1978 under the guidance of Bernard Takawira for whom he worked for four years. He now lives and works in Harare. Shamuyarira has exhibited regularly in Zimbabwe and also in Europe, North America and Australia.

Bernard Takawira
Hunter changing into Kudu 1988

BERNARD TAKAWIRA

Born in 1945 in Nyanga, Bernard Takawira began sculpting after leaving school in 1967. While at agricultural college he spent holidays sculpting at Vukutu, in Nyanga, where Frank McEwen had established a sculpture community (the Vukutu Workshop) and where Bernard's brother John also worked. After graduating from college Bernard Takawira spent seven years as an agricultural advisor while continuing to sculpt in his spare time.

Now living on his own farm at Bromley near Harare, Takawira continues to develop as a sculptor. His early work tended to roundness and strong forms, though since 1982/83 unsculpted rough surfaces have come to predominate. This later work, while still generally utilising the hard black serpentine and springstone he prefers, has a textural emphasis which takes advantange of unworked surfaces and the outer oxidised blanket of stone. A sculptor of international repute he has exhibited in Africa, Britain, New Zealand, Sweden, Italy, Austria and other countries.

John Takawira
Skeletal Man 1969

JOHN TAKAWIRA

Born in 1938, John Takawira grew up in Nyanga and was educated at Mount Mellersay Mission School. He was introduced to stone

Lazarus Takawira
Water Spirit 1989

Gladman Zinyeka
Murume (Husband) 1989

carving by his uncle, Joram Mariga, and as one of the first members of the National Gallery Workshop School was greatly encouraged by Frank McEwen. Often considered to be the doyen of the movement in Zimbabwe he was greatly respected by aspiring artists and throughout his life consistently attempted to break new ground both in imagery and technique. Honoured in his own country and abroad he exhibited extensively in many parts of the world and has sculpture in many important collections. Prior to his untimely death in 1989 he was considered by artists and critics to be one of the most significant artists to emerge from Zimbabwe.

LAZARUS TAKAWIRA

Born 1952 in Nyanga. He comes from a strong sculptural background. His uncle is Joram Mariga and he is the brother of John and Bernard Takawira.

Takawira became a full time sculptor in 1980 and was associated with the Vukutu workshop on a part-time basis until 1984. He now lives in Harare, has exhibited extensively in many countries and has work in important collections.

GLADMAN ZINYEKA

Born in 1962 in the Gutu district of Zimbabwe. The War of Independence was at its peak during Zinyeka's formative years. After independence, aged twenty one , he moved to Chitungwiza, the second largest conurbation in Zimbabwe where he continues to live and work. He started to make sculpture in 1986 and after a short period with Samson Kuvhengurwa he worked on his own.

Zinyeka's work is inspired by early experiences and his environment. Through stone he expresses the individual dilemmas of urban and rural life.He has exhibted in Zimbabwe, London and New Zealand and his work is beginning to be acquired for important collections.

Opposite:
Joseph Muzondo
The Last Warrior 1989

Bernard Takawira
A Woman's Anguish 1988

YORKSHIRE
SCULPTURE PARK
BRETTON HALL
WEST BRETTON
WAKEFIELD
WEST YORKSHIRE
WF4 4LG
ADMINISTRATION 0924 830579
INFORMATION 0924 830302